AQUARIUS
HOROSCOPE 2015

Lisa Lazuli

ABOUT THE AUTHOR

Lisa Lazuli studied astrology with the Faculty of Astrological Studies in London.

She has practiced since 1999.

Lisa has been a regular guest on BBWM and BBC Shropshire talking about astrology and doing both horoscopes and live readings. She has also made guest appearances on Fox FM, BBC Cambridgeshire, BBC Northamptonshire, BBC Coventry and Warwickshire and US Internet Radio Shows including the Debra Clement Show.

Lisa wrote horoscopes for Asian Woman Magazine.

Now available in eBook and paperback:

TAURUS: Your Day, Your Decan, Your Sign *The most REVEALING book on The Bull yet.* Includes 2015 Predictions.

ARIES HOROSCOPE 2015

TAURUS HOROSCOPE 2015

GEMINI HOROSCOPE 2015

CANCER HOROSCOPE 2015

LEO HOROSCOPE 2015

VIRGO HOROSCOPE 2015

LIBRA HOROSCOPE 2015

SCORPIO HOROSCOPE 2015

SAGITTARIUS HOROSCOPE 2015

CAPRICORN HOROSCOPE 2015

Lisa Lazuli is also the author of

The mystery/thrillers:

A Sealed Fate

Holly Leaves

Next of Sin

As well as:

Delicious, Nutritious Recipes for the Time and Cash Strapped

Paleo Diet: Get Started, Get Motivated, Feel Great.

99 ACE Places to Promote Your Book

Pressure Cooking Reinvented.

FOREWARD

Dear Reader,

I hope my yearly horoscopes will provide you with some insightful guidance during what is a very tricky time astrologically speaking with the heavy planets i.e. Pluto and Uranus at loggerheads in cardinal signs and Neptune in Pisces calling us all to get in touch with our spiritual side.

I have a conversational style of writing; please excuse any grammatical errors, I write much as I would speak.

As the song goes, "Nobody said it was easy." I know the mass media pump-out shows us plenty about quick fix love, money, fame and success; however, life is a journey filled with challenges and obstacles designed to encourage us to find out what we are made of, and who we really are.

Embrace the good and bad and enjoy what is your unique experience.

Be the hero in your own personal life movie and never hide your spotlight.

I must add that the best astrology insights are gained from a unique chart based on your time, date, year and place of birth.

If you would like your natal chart calculated for FREE:

Click here: http://lisalazuli.com/2014/06/30/would-you-like-to-know-where-all-your-planets-are-free-natal-chart/

Please join me on Facebook:

https://www.facebook.com/pages/Lisa-Lazuli-Astrologer/192000594298158?ref=hl

Contents

"The bigger, the better in everything," and "Who dares wins!" are your mottos for the year.

Aquarians are known for being ahead of their time and for thinking out of the box when it comes to life, philosophy, society and love. This year you are bolder than ever in your quest for honesty, truth and integrity, and you aim to bring those qualities into each part of your personal and professional life. You are thinking big and aiming high, and it is definitely a case of 'nothing ventured nothing gained': failure will not put you off trying new things as you regard anything you attempt as a success independent of the outcome. You are willing to take risks and put yourself on the line for what you believe in. This is an exciting year of taking up challenges and evolving in interesting directions in terms of personal growth – it is not about humdrum routine, but education and enlightenment.

2015 is certainly a year to get started on projects and plans which you have shelved or held back on. You have a very optimistic attitude now, which will embolden you to go for things and to tackle both physical and emotional challenges. This is the year to start dating again; take up golf again; start getting involved in social groups again. We all have knock backs from time to time (health-wise, emotionally, financially etc.), which may discourage us from doing things we once enjoyed – but 2015 is a bounce back year when it is time to get right back on the horse again in terms of the things which you enjoy.

This is an excellent year for new business ventures as you have foresight and quite a measure of vision – you can rely on support and encouragement from those closest to you, and you may find a partner in this venture who you will really enjoy working with.

You are encouraged this year to go that extra mile in whatever you do, even if it's risky or has a small chance of success – somehow that next step is so enticing you have to challenge yourself to do it, and you can be successful. I do not suggest you take gambles that are crazy and ill- advised, but I think you will not be able to help yourself in biting off that little extra and going for broke. This is not a year of being cautious and holding back – Aquarians are jumping right in at the deep end and embracing the unknown with a "What the hell" attitude. Life tends to come alive when we take chances – when we live well within our limits and never push boundaries, life can be boring and humdrum, but when we put ourselves on the line, take chances and resolve to have no regrets, things tend to happen for the better, even if they do not happen exactly as we have planned.

Whether it be money, sporting success and achievement, academic achievement or social prestige you go after this year, what is more important are the experiences and what you learn about yourself along that way. 2015 marks a big learning curve in terms of yourself and who you are – we are not the job we have, the awards we get, the money we have etc., we are so much more than that and yet this year, via the vehicles of money, success or study, something about you and what you stand for and believe in will be revealed.

It may be that you have never had a strong feeling about philosophy, religion or the meaning of life, but events this year will both test and direct your faith. If you do have strong philosophical views about life, you may well question your views and develop new or more refined views that will impact on your life.

Expansion is certainly what 2015 is about, and that can mean your waistline as well – you are not especially disciplined and will tend to throw caution to the wind when it comes to both alcohol and food. This need not be an entirely bad thing, as we all need to let our hair down at times and to let go of the strict protocols that we have laid down or perhaps even which others have laid down for us. There is something liberating about not following your own rules for once and just saying, "What the hell!" 2015 is a reaction against anything that restricts, binds and limits you. Beliefs, people, groups, jobs and anything else that holds you hostage to a routine that stifles your spirit will have to go! You will strive to re-shape your life in a way in which you as a person are free again – Aquarians are free spirits, you are a law unto yourself, you are peaceful people, but you must have freedom of thought and freedom to express yourself. 2015 will make you think more about stagnation and restriction in your life and how you can free yourself and your spirit again; you will rebel against the institutions or people who are suppressing the real you.

Spontaneity and learning are very important, and you will be constantly seeking stimulation – you will find it hard to focus on routine and mundane matters and will attempt to add creativity and original flair into whatever you do. This year is fabulous for those in the arts or creative fields as you are original and flamboyant and will attract attention – a good breakthrough year for aspiring artists (in fashion, acting, dance, design etc) as you have the power to get that first important break.

Self-employed Aquarians can see their business really take off this year – you can benefit from a combination of foresight and courage, which will help you to not only seize opportunity, but know how to make the most of it. Aquarians in jobs where you have a degree of autonomy and can make independent decisions, can shine and will gain recognition for both your achievements and ideas. Aquarians who work where they have no freedom and are heavily supervised, may throw their efforts into looking for something which better fulfils their needs; an unsatisfying job that is very materialistically driven and routine will have to go. For those of you in public service or who work in politics or charities where you have the ability to change the lives of others, you will be very opinionated and driven this year, and you may lock horns with others in terms of policy. In both your career and social life, you are idealistic and are motivated by high ideals and both material and non-material achievement. It is not all about the end result; it is the thrill of chasing an idea, making a plan become reality and then seeing what more can be done, what new target you can chase.

You will become distant from people who seek to control you or place limits on your expression; being true to yourself is more important than ever as is being true to principles. You will stand up for what you believe is right, even if that makes you unpopular or makes life difficult. Aquarians revel in being contrary, but this year you can use that fearlessness you have of not being agreed with or accepted to fight for causes and the rights of others. You will eventually win respect for being honest, above board and having a high-minded approach. This is a year when you can provide others with moral leadership and bring a certain wisdom and maturity to the table in any debate or issue. One downside of this year is that you may come across as arrogant or give over an impression of being intellectually superior or condescending. You do have to pay more attention to how you convey your message; you can win more people over to your side more quickly if you do not ride roughshod over opinions assuming you are always right. Actually, false assumptions can be your downfall this year – you are quick to act and quick to dismiss what does not suit you, you have to be a better listener and work more cooperatively with other people.

When things do not go your way, do not throw the baby out with the bathwater so to speak – stop, pause and think before you continue. 2015 has so many positives but getting carried away with yourself in a wave of your own propaganda, deaf to advice and warning signs can cause you to falter. At times, over-confidence and a complete neglect of detail are your downfalls. Thinking you have all the answers can cause you difficulties with authorities or superiors – check your facts and be clear and precise about figures and laws.

In one-to-one relationships there needs to be give and take and more quality listening from you. You need to make more of an effort to incorporate the ideas of those you live or work with. You are very opinionated and vocal about expressing your beliefs and ideas, but you can actually gain more followers if you show that you have respect for other people's ideas, as well – be more inclusive. You are prone to preaching tolerance and equality, but you do not always come across as very tolerant of anyone who disagrees with you, and you are not treating everyone else's ideas equally. You may think you are being very fair when you, in fact, are not, and you need to be aware of a certain self-delusion – are you seeing and appreciating how you are coming across to others? Trying to see yourself through the eyes of others can be difficult, and yet you must try so that you can refine your approach. These factors are especially relevant in love and romance.

You want to be mentally challenged this year and will enjoy debate – study itself may bore you, and you can learn far more from discussing and debating with others. If you are in school or uni, form study groups where you exchange and toss about ideas as you will learn faster that way.

Aquarians can be very effective in crisis situations this year and if you work in A&E, as a paramedic, in fire and rescue or in any career which brings you into dangerous or emotionally explosive situations, you can react and coordinate others with an amazing clarity of mind and objectivity.

Aquarians are romantics at heart and not just in the Cupid sense. You have a romantic view of life and people, and this is part of your idealistic nature: this year you are especially romantic in your approach to life and the way you pursue your goals. This can give you inspiration and allow you to draw an enjoyment from what you do in a way which makes this year special. It can, however, also leave you open to attack or deception as you are too trusting and perhaps not sceptical enough of others who may manipulate your good intentions. You really do need to get those rose-coloured specs off and take a 'cold light of day' look at things and people.

In love, you are very idealistic and truly want to escape into a love bubble. This is a wonderful year to fall in love as you are in the right frame of mind to fall into the warm embrace of someone you care for and enjoy a classic romance with all the magic that comes with falling in love. Love is a form of escapism, it is a place where we can lose the world and suddenly experience a drug which is totally legal – that is where Aquarians want to be this year and so go ahead, "Birds do it, bees do it, even educated fleas do it … let's fall in love!"

The one danger is that you may fall in love with someone who is unattainable or who you become infatuated with in a game of unrequited love. While you are ready to bond with someone special on a deep intimate and spiritual level that does not mean you can be unrealistic, you must be discerning and careful about who you give your heart to. It is possible that Aquarians may fall for someone who they think can save or redeem and that may cost you more emotionally than it gives you back – you cannot let a lover or potential lover drain you emotionally in the name of love, you have to have boundaries, and you have to protect yourself.

Aquarians will make sacrifices for the one they love this year: you may move to be closer to your new partner; you may change jobs so that you can spend more time with your wife/husband; you may sacrifice your own happiness to make your partner happy – yet this sacrifice is not about being a martyr, it does give you a deep sense of oneness with your partner and can bring you closer than ever and so it is a sacrifice worth making.

Health-wise, you must ensure you get plenty of sleep and avoid stimulants and anything artificial. This is not the year to burn the candle at both ends, and you need rest, solitude and mental breathers to keep healthy, mentally and physically. You must eat more green vegetables and fresh fruit and keep your body acidity down (i.e. be more alkaline) by eating less processed food and red meat.

2015 is an amazing year artistically, and you will be inspired and supremely creative. You can tap into the collective unconscious and create works of art that capture the public mood and convey the message of a generation.

Many Aquarians will travel abroad to take an active part in humanitarian endeavors i.e. Ebola care, aid to refugees, aid to those affected by freak climatic events and other such missions. Your view is very global right now, and you have a strong need to make a difference to something in the world or society. Even if you stay at home, you can be very involved in direct action and political activism.

An extraordinarily interesting and growth orientated time. A year of material and esoteric development and success with new parameters set in your life and a fresh opportunity to be who you are.

LIFE

You will have to pay careful attention to how you project yourself and how you communicate in order to ensure that the right message hammers home. Complacency about the level of understanding of others or haste in the way you explain things can lead to miscommunications and thus failures and hiccoughs in your business and personal life. Be clear and be calm; you tend to be a little jumpy and presumptuous this month, and you really do have to take a step back and have a good look over things.

January is a busy month, where you will feel both motivated and stimulated by the things you are doing, but not everything will run to plan, leading to stress and last minute changes of mind and plan. This is not the time to be dogmatic on any matter as sudden changes or new information may force you to change a strongly held view. The best thing to do is to not be scared to change your mind and change direction: it's OK, changing your mind is not admitting defeat, it is just being adaptable and dynamic.

Whether it is a contract, an essay, a speech or a proposal, check it and check it again and do not be so hasty to finish it that you leave messy details unclarified.

This is a month of things coming unstuck – problems you thought were resolved will crop up again, and this time you really will have to deal with them in order to put them to bed. Coughs and head colds may also hamper your ability to work at the pace you would like.

If you have not stuck to your New Year resolutions (which is highly probably given the nature of this month) do not despair, the best thing to do is cancel your resolutions and begin them again next month.

Busy and hectic, January is an exciting time of new starts and promising new contacts socially and professionally – some of these may take a while to bear fruit, patience is needed.

LOVE

Relationships are very important to you this month, and you are eager to chat and engage intellectually with your loved one. Intellectual stimulation and loyalty are the most important things to an Aquarian, and in January you really want to get that banter and witty conversation going.

You will be the one to take the lead in your relationship whether that is deciding on what you do on the weekend or initiating lovemaking.

You are feeling able to talk to your partner about more serious matters as well, i.e. money and the household finances – this is an ideal time to agree on a budget or talk about how to save. You are very persuasive right now, and that is ideal if you are eager to convince your partner to do or buy something. You may have discussions about your mutual friends or your social groups, and you may decide to distance yourselves from certain people you were both once close to.

A great month for a romantic surprise or wedding proposal.

A very promising month for new relationships as you are so perky, charming and willing to engage about romantic matters. Aquarians are very receptive to love, and that creates the ideal atmosphere for Cupid to strike. You have quite an air of self-confidence and warmth about you which is very attractive.

CAREER

Cultivating relationships is vital; do not try and run before you can walk in terms of your new associates or potential business colleagues. You need to spend time evaluating and analyzing who and/or what you'll be dealing with very closely before you commit. You should also take a softly softly approach rather than an all guns blazing approach to new projects, especially if they are with a new associate or client. If anything is an unknown quantity in your work life, treat it with caution and do your research before you commit to it.

If you are diversifying or are in a new job, do not be afraid to take your time and find your feet – do not allow yourself to be rushed.

This is a very good time for detailed market analysis and research – but you must be systematic and not ignore statistics and research which does not suit you.

In any workplace there are known unknowns and unknown unknowns, and this month it is the unknown unknowns which are the problem – these include random events and problems you could not have foreseen, and this is exactly why a steady and cautious approach is needed. If you press on too fast, you may be more exposed to these random events. This is also why you should proceed with caution with any new client, new supplier or new piece of software as when you are new to something there are by definition more unknowns.

Aquarians involved in children's entrainment, toy making/selling, international trade, copy write law and the tourism industry can do very well this month.

LIFE

A month of feathers in your cap and the feeling of motoring after having stalled. After the changes of mind and confusion of last month, you have a clear road ahead of you and can plan and move forward on your aims and goals. After a few refinements and adjustments last month that were irritating, you are actually better placed than before.

This month the law and government regulations can actually be rather helpful to you, and they may help you solve a problem or get resolution on an issue – I would advise seeking legal advice or contacting your local MP/Senator about any problems you have as they may have some practical advice on how to address things. Make more use of free citizen advice centers or bureaus who may know more about laws and regulations than you. There are ways to access the law without having to spend lots of money – research how you can use these.

You are well organized this month and will be able to plan even complex matters effectively. A very good time to take your finances, paperwork or PC filing systems into hand – get rid of rubbish, save anything important and file things more systematically. Often life is so busy that we forget how important storing info and important documents is.

Later this month, you will have a burst of energy which can help you to be very productive with practical things – so if you have DIY, renovating, carpentry, gardening or anything physically demanding to do, save it until then.

Firm friends will have good advice for you this month as well as being able to offer practical support and encouragement. Honesty and shared feelings will make a good friendship even more solid right now.

LOVE

Love is complex for Aquarians this month but also very rewarding. Aquarians enjoy puzzles; they love the unexplained, and the more enigmatic someone is, the more they are attracted. The more complicated and passionate a relationship is, even if it's a rocky road, the better as Aquarians will be fascinated and very involved. Aquarians love a chase, and they also love a person who has a vulnerable side.

Single Aquarians will be very attracted to a person who they see as either 'damaged' or with issues – issues per se never scare a Water Bearer away. Aquarians have a need this year to act as a savior, and love is probably the ideal place to do this on a very intimate and personal level, and that is why Aquarians will attract challenging and demanding lovers, who can involve you in very deep and transformative relationships.

In existing relationships and marriages, you may stir things up quite unconsciously in order to take things to a new level by disrupting the equilibrium. You may be accused by your partner of looking for arguments, but you are really eager to get deeper conversation going. You need to find constructive ways of engaging with your partner about deeper and more sensitive subjects – don't be argumentative or create tension in order to get around to saying what is on your mind: perhaps read books or see movies that are about the topic you want to talk about and use that as a springboard.

This can be a very interesting Valentine's Day, especially if your partner shares your need for renewed intimacy and escapism – use your creativity to create that magic moment that cannot fail to impress your love. Sometimes Aquarians provoke passion in others as they are not able to easily access that passion themselves; this February use visualization to feel that passion and excitement within you – let go of the fear of losing your detachment.

CAREER

You are working very hard now to prove your worth: it is vital for you to show that you have the ability and you can take on any intellectual or creative challenge. You will work hard and be quite ingenious when it comes to making sure that you reach targets, get the grades or make the right impression. There is an 'in your face, that'll show you' attitude where you want to show your doubters that they have underestimated you. Often they say that the best revenge is success, and that is the theme this month.

You can work well with authority figures this month, and they may even help you. A friendship you develop with an older colleague or a person in your field with more experience than you can be very beneficial. Someone may take you under their wing this year and teach you a great deal, but you must be receptive as this will not necessarily be an easy relationship as this person will be hard to please and very exacting, but it is what you need.

The best lessons are the tough lessons – did you ever have a subject you struggled with at school, but once you got the hang of it you really got good at it? Sometimes we find a talent via hardship or struggle and that is why this year you must persist with difficult tasks or goals and not abandon them. The hardest things to get to grips with could be your greatest asset or skill long-term.

LIFE

The urge to be extravagant and to buy things which make you feel good is high right now, and yes, we all love some retail therapy, and what is wrong with enjoying yourself? However, make sure what you do spend on really does make you happy, and it is not a quick fix or a rush that leaves you feeling empty and unfulfilled later. You are after quick fixes this month, but you really do need to look inside and think about what you need for longer term satisfaction.

Aquarians are plagued in the early stages of this year with a need to prove themselves in ways that are not ultimately very nourishing: so what if everyone thinks you have a cool car or a designer label? When you are alone, do those same things that give you kudos make you happy? The things that make others happy and which other people value are not often the things which make the Aquarian happy – you are a maverick who must live to your own unique set of rules and values, things which make live valuable for you. So, be extravagant and spoil yourself this month by all means, but make sure you do it your way and on your own terms.

The solar eclipse this month can bring you a sense of self-belief and inner strength that will enable you to feel secure no matter what your financial outlook or stage of life. A sense of 'I can' and 'I will thrive and survive' is very strong right now, and that will propel you on with confidence. There is an ability within you right now to renew yourself at a very deep level.

LOVE

There is a strong sense of rediscovery this month – it is as if you have found yourself and reconnected with your core values and needs. This can make you an awesome partner to be with as you are radiating a glow of self-assurance. Other people respond to strength

– nothing wishy-washy inspires or motivates – your strength of mind and soul is good to be around.

It may well be that a new relationship or something that you are doing to help your partner has actually reawakened a part of you and has brought you a sense of purpose again.

We are so programmed in life to go after what we want, to be independent and to strive selfishly towards goals, that often the joy of being there for someone else or forgoing something so someone else can benefit is lost. This month in love you can find happiness in being happy for your partner and in being a cheerleader for him/her rather than just being about you.

This is also an excellent month for couples with shared goals who work as a team. If you do not have shared goals, maybe that is what you are missing – find things to strive for as a couple and set targets: lose weight, save money, get fitter, take up a hobby, but do so together.

CAREER

If you have been struggling in your own business, this could be a turnabout month when things get better financially. There is a strong focus on resources, and if you run your own business or department, you need a root and branch review of how resources are allocated and used. It may be time to free up resources and outsource; maybe the wrong people are doing the wrong jobs and changing them about could improve efficiency. Look closely at your costs and also at how productive your assets are. Get rid of old cars or old machines that cost more to run and repair than new ones; perhaps lease instead of buying assets. Look at your assets and think about how to get more from them.

Ego and financial status or material wealth are very much connected this month, and you do not want to make a bad financial decision because your ego got in the way – which is why caution is needed as some decisions may be ego not fact driven.

In careers where you work in a job, think about skills you have which you are not using and try and get your employer to give you more work in the fields you are best at or trained in. Speak to your HR department about moving within your company or look for roles where you are freer to use your initiative.

This is a very positive money month, and you may find a lucrative second income stream from something you can do on weekends or evening – perhaps it is a hobby or language skill you have which others want and will pay for.

LIFE

Aquarians are not instinctive, in fact, you prefer to act in accordance with reason and critical evaluation, but this month you can be rather emotionally and instinctively driven. Often your impulsive reactions to a situation are in contrast to what you consciously aimed to do, and the result can mean you taking a different direction quite suddenly. Emotions and irritations can flare up quite quickly from nowhere, and it will be hard for you to keep a lid on them. You can be rather defensive and touchy right now, and this is not a good time for cool-headed decision-making. This is, however, a good month for dealing with things which have actually been bugging you for a while – it's like you finally have the oomph to just knock things on the head and when you have done so you will feel like, "Phew, why did I not do this before!"

Family are important to you this month, and you may travel to visit your family and hometown – but more than that, your visit will entail you making a practical effort towards fixing or rebuilding something, be it something physical or a broken relationship. This effort you make, whether it is a purely practical job or something more to do with repairing human bonds, will enable you to feel far better about yourself and more focused. It may be a case of having to put your pride in your pocket when it comes to an individual dispute you have within your family for the greater good of the family as a whole.

There is something nagging this month, something you know you should do, but are putting off – this may make you irritable and cranky (as mentioned in paragraph 1) – the best thing is to deal with the issue head on, or as in the 2nd paragraph, throw your efforts/energy into doing something constructive, especially if that relates to home or family to work off the tension.

You may invest in your home via an extension, redecorating or a new kitchen.

LOVE

Private and passionate is the theme in love – you are more likely to be private about expressing affection i.e. you may act cool towards your partner in public, but behind the scenes at home you are red hot and ready to go.

You can be quite snappy this month, but you will be quick to apologize, which means that any argument and ill feeling will blow over fast.

This is a very good month for new same-sex partnerships – you may decide to move in together and make a commitment. Same sex couples will enter a new phase of togetherness and things will get much deeper with a firm understanding that defies words.

Single Aquarians will feel a strong yearning to be in a relationship, and thus they will heavily engage in social activities with the opposite sex in order to meet a potential partner. You may meet someone who already has children, and you will be ready to embrace that happily. In new relationships, this is the month when Aquarians will feel accepted and assimilated into the family of their lover.

CAREER

A strong link between finances and creativity means that there is money to be made in the arts and entertainment, and also if you are able to be creative financially, i.e. in the way you invest and the timing in which you buy/sell stocks and shares. You may well profit from stocks in mining, building and the sports industries.

You should spend most of the first part of the month travelling in order to see clients, do business and make purchases – this may include trade fairs and meeting with suppliers. Logistical matters are also important to attend to. However, the second half of the month will be focused on production and working from your desk, getting everything organized. You may be able to do work from home in order to get more done and be more productive. You may have to spend time in libraries doing research and perhaps looking through archived information for research purposes.

This is a good month to deal with real estate sales and transfers, investment in real estate or investment in geological research.

Take note of environmental law and regulations and make sure you comply. In some cases, Aquarians may be instrumental in paving the way for more Green Regulation or Green awareness via activism and blogging.

LIFE

There is a need to get to the bottom of things – you have a nagging doubt that things are not as they seem this month, and that is making you uneasy. Dealing with people may be harder than usual as you do not have that element of trust, and thus you are holding back.

You will tend to be secretive and not to speak you mind (when it comes to revealing your plans and strategies) – you may play your cards close to your chest, choosing to only convey what you have to.

There is strange dynamic to this month where you may act out the subconscious anger of the group – we all know a situation where everyone is thinking something, but you say it and then get criticized. Part of your gift this month is being the one to speak about taboos and to be brave enough to say what should be said. While this may seem to backfire in the short run, in the long term you will be respected, and more and more will come forward saying they agree. Aquarians are known for breaking down barriers of thought, and you know what happens when anything breaks? There is a crash and a smash, and then we clear up and get on with it – ignore the short-term disruption and know that you acted with truth and honesty.

You should not be scared to stand apart from the crowd this May, in fact, it is the best way to go, and blindly following would be the wrong course of action. We have all had that situation where everyone was doing something, and yet we got the blame for it – beware of that happening and do not be inured into doing something simply because others are doing it and getting away with it – you may be the one to be singled out and made an example of.

One way or another you will be center stage this month, and so make sure that you are picked out for something that you are proud of.

LOVE

Relationships can be tricky this month as you are giving mixed signals – you are saying one thing, but you are projecting something different and your loved one or those close to you may be reacting to what you are projecting rather than what you are saying and that can add to your confusion. We all underestimate the amount of animal intuition we use to interpret the actions of others, especially those close to us. Sometimes we are almost unaware that we are picking up vibes or giving them out – this month you are giving out some rather intense vibes without realizing it, and you can be conveying a certain hostility, even if you are saying something positive.

Be more aware of what you are thinking when you are speaking – if you are thinking about something that is troubling you at work while you compliment your wife/husband's outfit – the wife/husband may pick up the negative thoughts instead of the positive comment.

You will also be more attuned to the signals your partner is giving out, and this may be a very powerful way of helping them to open up about a secret worry or problem they are carrying. You are rather psychic right now and used with sensitivity and awareness this can increase deeper understanding in the relationship. You should get into some quality and meaningful, intimate conversations – undisturbed (take the phones off and get the kiddies to bed) – as you can share great heart-to-hearts right now.

CAREER

Stand by your opinions, and do not be swayed by the crowd, especially if you work in scientific or technical fields. You have a very good feel for your subject right now and can make deductions and associations that others may not see. This is a month when you are feeling very innovative and inventive, and if allowed scope, you can have a big impact and make some significant advancements.

May is especially good for Aquarians who work in cutting-edge industries or artistic fields where one needs to be on trend and current. It's a good time for lateral thinking and throwing out the rule book, go with your instincts.

Business travel may be spur of the moment and so make sure that you are not over-committed this month – you want to leave yourself free to take up sudden opportunities that can arise. It is a month of surprises and one off offers and chances to do new things. You can be known – in whichever job you are in – for your original thinking and astute analysis of complex data: be it financial, technical or socio-psychological data.

Aquarians who write on mind/body spirit type subjects or who teach new-age subjects can be highly inspired in delivering their message and making advancements in these fields.

LIFE

This is a month when things come together for friendship and fun – if you have been trying to get your friends all together for a good time out and everyone has been busy or occupied, now is the month when all your plans for fun, recreation and entertainment come together. You may manage to nab those tickets for a hot concert or perhaps a sporting event which you have been itching to attend.

The creative juices are flowing, which will also assist you in completing any creative or arty projects which you have. You may travel to compete in sport, and you are very strategically minded, which is great for sports that have a strong mental element.

This is also a very productive and successful month for Aquarians who are analytical, and who are required to solve complex problems with maths or who need to scour legal documents for key clauses.

It is vital to retain focus this month and to follow through on the projects and chores which are most essential and have the most chance of success. If you have time later, you can come back to the avenues which looked interesting and that are worth experimenting with. What you should not be saying to yourself is, "I really should be doing A, but B looks rather interesting, never tried B before, might have a little go at that!" Go for what you know works i.e. A first and then come back to B if resources and time permit. By all means, do not neglect to pursue something you have set your heart on, but it may have to wait on the backburner this month.

LOVE

Flattery will get you everywhere this June if you use it advisedly. You are very keen to spend quality time with your partner, and you are showing that you appreciate him/her, and this will get the romantic juices flowing. You are idealistic in relationships now and will be overlooking the trivial matters to focus on what really counts deep down. It is the fundamental togetherness and the quirks and nuances of the relationship which are exciting you this month – the way you interact, compliment and act as foils to each other's personality is especially relevant to you. You can really benefit and learn from the differences and different strengths your partner has as opposed to you.

This is not a month when you will want to be alone or go off on your own to do things; you want to be with your partner or lover as much as possible and share experiences together. If your partner is away or you are single, you will feel rather lonely and may be constantly texting or Skyping him/her, and if you are single you will be ringing up friends to go out socially.

For single Aquarians, this is a wonderful month to start a promising new romance. All Aquarians are feeling rather empty when they are alone, you have a strong need to be part of a pair and have someone with you to relate to and bounce ideas off – if alone you may feel isolated and moody. Relationships and doing things with your partner (new or old) is the tonic you need right now.

CAREER

There is a strong focus on working with children this month – it may be in a coaching role, as a teacher or fighting for the rights of children. You can arouse interest and help youngsters gain confidence via sports or other games of skill. Working with kids can also be a great deal of fun and could possibly earn you a second income.

If you are a sportsperson or fitness trainer this month, technique and following protocols is very important as is diet – do not take risks with supplements, stimulants or even prescription medicines which you have not used before.

In office situations, watch your back as sexual jealousy could cause someone to act in a way that may be a problem for you. Do not discuss personal matters with colleagues this month and keep emotion separate from your work.

Speculation and hasty financial decisions could be a bad move and so delay and think twice before signing any cheques.

A very interesting month for those who work in metallurgy, with chemicals, in pharmacy or energy especially if you work in R&D. Also, an excellent month for physiotherapists and chiropractors as your ability to heal with your hands is enhanced.

LIFE

Keeping promises and being discreet is very important this month. You have to know when the truth is actually not what is needed, and you must respect the deeper issues at stake.

You may have to be rather controlled and disciplined this month, and getting what you want will need some sacrifice and hard work – you may have to forgo something you really would love to buy in order to save money, or perhaps you will need to pass up an opportunity to socialize in order to put in more work at the office. Finances will tend to dictate your life somewhat this month, but you need to stay focused on the goal as you can make some excellent progress workwise.

You are taking obligations and responsibility very seriously right now, in fact, you are in a rather serious and single-minded frame of mind, which is a very good thing as you can achieve and impress others. You may find yourself in control of funds, i.e. a trust fund, estate, as a treasurer or as a purser.

You may have to become an expert in some aspect of the law this month in order to resolve an issue at work or a domestic one – your own research and ability to find nuggets of important detail within swathes of rubbish can be critical.

LOVE

This month, events at work will impact on your marriage or relationship – it may be a new position leads to more hours or that your new job involves more travel away from home. Study or coursework to do with a promotion may also eat into your private time. Adjustments to your personal life will happen due to work or career, but they can be positive as well in the longer terms, and you need to focus on these.

Loyalty and being able to count on the support of your partner is vital to you – the more he/she understands your needs and stresses, the better the relationship will be. However, if your partner is unwilling to be cooperative and understanding, this can lead to frostiness in the bedroom and long periods of silence. This month is a challenge in terms of how you both communicate and express yourselves emotionally – strong relationships will come through, and you will feel even closer, while shaky relationships with no depth of feeling or mutual compassion will suffer. This month will test your commitment and how much you both care. July will test whether you can work as a team or whether you are both selfish and in it for the good times only.

New relationships that are based on superficial feelings will flounder right now while relationships with potential will become more committed.

CAREER

If you work in partnership, you may find the relationship with your partner/s strained and difficult, especially due to creative differences or disagreements on how to allocate resources. It will take both diplomacy and some tongue biting to smooth things over, and you will have to be highly flexible in terms of how you work this month. You may also find the work ethic of those you work with disappointing, and you may find that you are picking up the pieces and doing extra work due to their indifference. You need to find ways of motivating them without coming across as a taskmaster. Politics within your firm or industry or career can be very annoying and even offensive to your strong principles and sense of equality – it is best not to rock the boat in the short run as you may have more scope to change things later this year.

Corporate finances, tax and insurances are the key areas in which you may experience frustration and some disagreement this month – these issues may hold up progress towards goals you have set, and you may have to hire an expert to help you to understand the facts and rules better. Do not under any circumstances be tempted to exaggerate an insurance claim – be cautious with submission of paperwork.

LIFE

There is a tendency to go a little overboard this month – yes the foodaholic and shopaholic within is just waiting to go crazy. But, hey it's August, which means that in the Northern Hemisphere most people are in holiday mood and ready to let their hair down. This is a really good month to indulge, be lazy and spoil yourself. Lady Luck is shining her light on you, and you have this good feeling that everything is well with the world, and things are working out. After last month, which was a little serious, you need some light relief, as long as you do not go overboard: remember too much of a good thing is also bad.

So, this is a very good month for having fun and for spending quality time with those you care about. Travel is certainly possible, but it may turn out differently to what you had expected. This is certainly a fun month, and yet the real enjoyment often comes from things you did not expect, and sometimes the things you highly anticipated disappoint somewhat. It can be a surprising months of letdowns countered by lovely surprises – the key is moderation and managing expectations. What this month is trying to teach you is that joy often lies in surprising places and that excesses of food, drink or retail are often poor substitutes for real contentment and pleasure.

You are very kind and generous right now and will help anyone – you must be discerning though!

LOVE

In general, this is a very good month for love and sex due to your bonhomie and general positivity which you are radiating. Kind, generous and light-hearted, you are fun to be with and that aids both new and established relationships. This is an ideal time to smooth over any lingering bad feeling and take the relationship forward in a positive way.

One thing to take note of: you must know when to stop. What I mean by that is that you are prone to going overboard i.e. too much teasing, too much partying, too much joking about, over exertion, etc. Your sense of proportion is somewhat dimmed, and you may misjudge another person's feelings … know when the party is over, and your partner wants some sleep. Try to be more sensitive to your partner's moods, feelings and desires.

One negative aspect of this month is that you can lose a grip of yourself and become overbearing or even diva-ish, giving off an arrogance that is off -putting. You should just be yourself, don't try too hard to fit in, be funny or be center of attention – being your tolerant, interesting, free spirited Aquarian self is brilliant enough.

Your sex life can be amazing this month – make sure your partner is fulfilled and do not be afraid to work at the sex! Yes, it can be terrific sex, but that does not mean you don't have to work at it, refine and perfect it. So be creative with sex.

CAREER

You should have some success with the matters of finance, taxes, insurance etc., which were bothering you last month.

Teams and partnerships will require great effort and focus, and you will have to strike a balance between offering leadership while not actually taking the lead – while the team needs direction you will have to be clever about how you persuade and cajole the rest into following up on your ideas.

You may begin this month the task of applying for loans for long-terms projects. Students may be working hard to secure enough finance to attend the university of their choice; businesses may be looking for loan deals so that they can expand. Either way, you should not be deterred by the challenge as if you are organized and positive you can get the money you need to work on your dream.

There is a strong theme of putting plans into place so that you can make a concerted effort to pursue some goal of deep importance to you – the will within you to make this move is very powerful, and your ability to put the practical parts in place is there.

LIFE

You can achieve both recognition and/or fame from something you write this month; be it a book, blog post, article or research paper. You can strike on something that is very important and relevant.

Learning is especially exciting now if you are a student as what you will learn will seem especially crucial to understanding current events in the world. Aquarians are very engaged with the world right now, and you are more interested than usual in current events, economics and politics as you can see how they have an impact on your life. You may be inspired to get more involved by seeking out people with similar opinions or getting involved in activism. You can be a role model or torch bearer for new ways of thinking; be inspiring but do be careful of not forcing your views on others when you get all fired up.

Aquarians are loving their gadgets and gizmos this month, and you will be an early adopter when it comes to new technology – i.e. when I see the queue outside Apple for the new pad or phone, or whatever, I know it'll be you guys.

You have a strong need to regenerate this month. That could mean a good clear-out of the attic so that you can turn it into a new room or office. It may mean getting rid of your rickety old shed at the garden bottom or on a more psychological level it means that you are ready to get to grips with something buried in your head, something you usually do not speak of or avoid dealing with. You may want to conquer a phobia or confront a fear head-on. You may undergo some psychology to resolve an issue especially to do with guilt. You may begin to tackle feelings of grief or loss, which you have never wanted to face up to before – this process can be revealing and rejuvenating.

LOVE

If you don't know what you want, it can be hard to get it – fluctuating moods and psychological needs can make it hard for you to understand yourself, which can impact on relationships. However, as the month goes on, you will feel more comfortable and settled within yourself, and you will become quite amorous.

Sensuality and touch are more important to you, and you can become aroused very quickly by touch and aroma. You will need quite a bit of sex this September, and it is not just about the sex, but the hugs and affection.

New relationships can begin very fast, and it may not be long before they get intimate. Due to relationships moving so fast, you must be discriminating as due to your desire you may not be as discreet as you should. Avoid office romances or affairs that could leave a nasty taste after the passion dies down.

CAREER

This is a very important month for academics and policy makers (in government, local government, school PTA's etc.) – you have the ability to shape the lives of others via the rules you play a role in drawing up, or via the ideas you are putting out there. You may be the first or one of the first to adopt a new method or new technological advancement which can take your industry by storm.

Gut feel is very important in your business dealings, especially when you have to make decisions about unknowns, i.e. how will the economy be doing in six months' time; what will happen to exchange rates etc. You can be highly perceptive and accurate in making long-term forecasts and projections where there are many uncertain variables.

You also have a keen insight into your competitors' motivations this month, and that can allow you to act swiftly and decisively. When I say competitors, I also mean those colleagues who you compete against for promotion or meeting targets. You are very shrewd right now and can outwit the others.

Your work (as a social worker, psychologist, lawyer, nurse, doctor etc.) may bring you into contact with people who are outcast from society in some way i.e. criminals, mentally ill, homeless, illegal immigrants etc. to a larger degree than usual. You will get a very clear insight into their point of view, which may change some of your opinions, and you may be inspired to raise awareness and try and help in some way.

LIFE

This is very much a university of life graduation month – you will learn something very important regardless of whether it is at university, school or within the course of everyday life. You may actually be overwhelmed with information, or information you do receive can knock you sideways as it was not what you had assumed or anticipated.

Your beliefs will also be tested: it is not so much practicing what you preach, but believing your own dogma i.e. if you are teaching your children about religion, but you have doubts yourself, you will not be able to make them believe. If you are teaching students a certain technique or method and you do not believe it yourself, they will pick up on that distrust you have and will not be successful with that method. It's not just about what you say and what you do – you have to really believe in it 100% to sell it to others.

You have to grapple with some self-doubt this month – you really need to give yourself a thorough pep talk and clamp down any negative voices in your head. Life always tests our level of self-belief and a dip in self-confidence is a good opportunity to focus on positives – write the positive and negatives down and take practical steps to get on top of those negatives.

LOVE

A lover or someone you meet romantically may have a very powerful effect on you in a way that you act quite out of character. You may find you argue passionately with this person, and you disagree about everything, yet they intrigue you and almost have a spell over you. This kind of romance can be intoxicating and exciting for an Aquarian, and it can be rather successful in the short term – in the long term you may find you have more in common that you thought.

Arguments over the joint bank account or your debt may pepper marriages, and it is best to be honest – do not hide the bank statement, just admit you purchased those shoes or that golf club. This is also a time of disagreement regarding the rules and boundaries you set for your children. It may be hard to compromise as you may have ideologically different views – perhaps you can come up with a mixed approach incorporating both your views.

You are feeling passionate this month, and that passion can translate into great sex or arguments as you are seeing things as black or white with no in-between. Your ego is the problem – it is the ego causing the arguments, so get your ego in check and "get down and make love!"

CAREER

This month it is very much trying to see the wood for the trees and not becoming so bogged down in detail that you lose sight of the bigger picture and the end goal. You need to trust your intuition, and you also need to have a measure of faith (be it faith in the universe, God or yourself) that you will make the right moves at the right time as it is just impossible to decide on logic and facts only. You may just have to go with something that doesn't really make sense but which feels right.

This is also a time where the more you look at something or research something, the more complicated it seems to get – perhaps you can only grasp it on an intuitive level. You also have to learn when to switch off and move on from things that are frustrating you.

Sweeping changes can happen right now within your business which can be very beneficial in terms of your financial situation and the way you work – it may be that a loan is approved or that a new tax break enables you to invest and expand.

LIFE

You will do your best to avoid conflict this month although you may still end up finding yourself in the middle of it. You will have to defend your ideas and goals against doubters. The problem for Aquarius right now is that you are open to having your actions influenced by others – other people can undermine your confidence or plans by being critical and pouring cold water on your ambitions – so the challenge is to distinguish constructive criticism from pure negativity. You need to surround yourself with upbeat and positive pro-active people as negative toxic people can drain you more than usual, and their attitude may bring you down.

This month, you are most motivated when pursuing goals that are close to your heart – you need to be emotionally involved in what you are doing or else you may go on tangents and lose concentration. It is a wonderful month to achieve in creative arts and in putting together entertainment events.

Hypnotherapy and neuro-linguistic programming can be useful devices for you to kick habits, get more motivated and overcome fear.

LOVE

This is a very mature and sensible time for relationships where you work well together and where respect and concern reign supreme. Things are consistent in relationships now, and while there may be less passion, there is a pleasant and warm feeling of togetherness. This is a very good time for those couples who work together within their career, and it is also a great time for couples to embark on projects together.

There is a strong sense of realism and perspective in your love life which will help you to make good decisions about the things that affect you both. You may both decide you need to get away from it all, and you may take off to a quiet log cabin, a place by the sea or something more exotic. There is a sense of you needing escapism and a chance to have almost a second honeymoon, just you two together remembering what it was like to fall in love. Unlike a honeymoon, this time it is more about friendship and being able to enjoy each other with no distractions.

New relationships are also going very well, especially relationships with large age gaps or long distance relationships. If you have just begun a relationship, a trip away together may really cement things.

CAREER

This is an excellent month for creative expression which involves movement, i.e. dance, mime, acrobatics and also for photography and cinematography – you have the ability to capture an idea or state of mind via the moving body or sets of images.

Actors, musicians, artists and those who work in the various support roles to theatre and film will have plenty of work. It is vital that those in creative fields promote themselves effectively via traditional media, social media and the grapevine as you have the potential to get seen and noticed right now, but you must have all the feelers out.

This month, think more about how you deliver speeches: the tone, style and rhythm are all important – read up about speech making and watch good speechmakers in action. You need to refine your way of communicating to be more effective and to have a dramatic effect – your content is excellent, but you need to be more creative about how you put information across.

November is very important for those who deal in international trade/import, especially if you import clothing, consumer goods, fabric or cosmetics – it is important to have your sales projections right as you need to be well-stocked.

LIFE

You need to be careful about your purchases this Christmas – yes, we all get excited, but all that glitters … you know the rest. Do be sure that you are not duped into what looks like an amazing offer, but which has hidden extras or hidden terms which you are not fully aware of – this is especially true for cell phone contracts, holidays, time share or broadband offers. Make sure that you can walk away and get a refund without incurring costs if you change your mind. Basically, think twice before you buy anything that is technical, comes with insurance or an onerous contract.

There are always times when we find out who our true friends are, and it is often over the holidays – you may get a sudden insight into the people you hang out with, which leaves you wondering if you really know them at all. It may be during a tipsy moment that something is revealed which makes you think – OK, I never knew that! You may take a step back from some friends, thereafter. A friend may actually be the catalyst for you having to deal with something you had either been put off or had been avoiding. Do be careful of getting into business or money lending situations with friends.

Look after your health this month – this is a very good time for a check-up and to take control of cholesterol, blood pressure and overall health issues. You should think about how to reduce stress and perhaps do some reading on how diet, meditation or exercise could reduce your stress levels for 2016. Pay more attention to health.

LOVE

This is a very good time for Aquarians (who have been in relationships for more than a year) to get married – there is a combination of tradition and magic in love that are ideal ingredients. It is not a good time for gunshot weddings – where you get married on the spur of the moment as you may not be thinking clearly.

Watch out for alcohol-induced liaisons which can come back to haunt you.

The spiritual side of relationships are vital to Aquarians who tire of the mundane and ordinary quickly and feel a need to examine feelings on a mystical level. Aquarians will enjoy deep conversations, and you will coax out the secrets and vulnerabilities of your partners with an empathy which is touching, and which will help a new or old relationship to reach a new level of intimacy and understanding. The key to good sexual and romantic relationships is being able to let go and drop your guard, not only expecting your partner to do so.

Aquarians may be disappointed with partners who fail to open up in a wholehearted way. You have very high expectations and your idealism can lead you to be disappointed in love, but like I said before, this year LOVE itself is an opportunity to learn more about yourself on an emotional level, and so instead of being disillusioned when things do not go as you imagined, do what you do best and analyze, understand, learn and grow. Unresolved issues to do with your mother figure may impact on how you relate to your partner – so be aware of triggers that reawaken childhood complexes.

CAREER

A very important month for word of mouth for those who work in the arts or the healing fields – if you have looked after your customers or clients well, this can be a very fortunate time financially when good karma brings you a rush of business.

This can be a very productive time for those training/working in any medical field – you can make big strides in your understanding and ability to diagnose.

You may sacrifice time over the holidays to devote to a job you are invested in – you will put your clients' or patients' well-being ahead of your self-interest, and this can lead to good karma as well as a great sense of personal achievement.

December is an excellent time for initiatives with similar businesses – these initiatives need not be all about selling, they may be charitable or humanitarian in nature, with positive spin offs.

This month is also fortunate for those of you who work with people in service industries – an empathy and compassion will allow you to give service that is outstanding and very helpful.

It is very important to track financial transactions, and shipping insurance is especially important. Do your bank reconciliations and keep an eye out for cheques that bounce. This is a very bad time for any risky scheme or venture – do not gamble.

THANK YOU SO MUCH FOR PUCHASING THIS BOOK – ALL THE VERY BEST FOR 2016!

CPSIA information can be obtained at www.ICGtesting.com
Printed in the USA
LVOW11s1551190215

427558LV00002B/346/P